Spring Harvest
Bible Workbook

ONE PEOPLE

Living Out God's Story

Elizabeth McQuoid

Authentic

LONDON · COLORADO SPRINGS · HYDERABAD

SPRING HARVEST

Equipping the Church for action

First Published in 2007 by Spring Harvest Publishing Division and Authentic Media

13 12 11 10 09 08 07   7 6 5 4 3 2 1

Authentic Media, 9 Holdom Avenue, Bletchley, Milton Keynes, Bucks., MK1 1QR
1820 Jet Stream Drive, Colorado Springs, CO 80921, USA
OM Authentic Media, Medchal Road, Jeedimetla Village, Secunderabad 500 055, A.P., India
www.authenticmedia.co.uk
Authentic Media is a division of Send the Light Ltd., a company
limited by guarantee (registered charity no. 270162)

British Library Cataloguing in Publication Data

A catalogue record for this book is available from the British Library

ISBN-13: 978-1-85078-758-7
ISBN-10: 1-85078-758-1

Typeset by Spring Harvest
Cover design by fourninezero design.
Print Management by Adare Carwin
Printed in Great Britain by J.H. Haynes & Co., Sparkford

CONTENTS

ABOUT THIS BOOK

This book is written primarily for a group situation, but can easily be used by individuals who want to study the plans God has for the church. It can be used in a variety of contexts, so it is perhaps helpful to spell out the assumptions that we have made about the groups that will use it. These can have a variety of names – home groups, Bible study groups, cell groups – we've used housegroup as the generic term.

- ▶ The emphasis of the studies will be on the application of the Bible. Group members will not just learn facts, but will be encouraged to think 'How does this apply to me? What change does it require of me? What incidents or situations in my life is this relevant to?'

- ▶ Housegroups can encourage honesty and make space for questions and doubts. The aim of the studies is not to find the 'right answer' but to help members understand the Bible by working through their questions. The Christian faith throws up paradoxes. Events in people's lives may make particular verses difficult to understand. The housegroup should be a safe place to express these concerns.

- ▶ Housegroups can give opportunities for deep friendships to develop. Group members can be encouraged to talk about their experiences, feelings, questions, hopes and fears. They can also offer one another pastoral support and get involved in each other's lives.

- ▶ There is a difference between being a collection of individuals who happen to meet together every Wednesday and being an effective group who bounce ideas off each other, spark inspiration and creativity, pooling their talents and resources to create solutions together: one whose whole is definitely greater than the sum of its parts. The process of working through these studies will encourage healthy group dynamics.

Space is given for you to write answers, comments, questions and thoughts. This book will not tell you what to think, but will help you discover the truth of God's word through thinking, discussing, praying and listening.

FOR GROUP MEMBERS

▶ You will probably get more out of the study if you spend some time during the week reading the passage and thinking about the questions. Make a note of anything you don't understand.

▶ Pray that God will help you to understand the passage and show you how to apply it. Pray for other members in the group too, that they will find the study helpful.

▶ Be willing to take part in the discussions. The leader of the group is not there as an expert with all the answers. They will want everyone to get involved and share their thoughts and opinions.

▶ However don't dominate the group. If you are aware that you are saying a lot, make space for others to contribute. Be sensitive to other group members and aim to be encouraging. If you disagree with someone, say so but without putting down their contribution.

FOR INDIVIDUALS

▶ Although this book is written with a group in mind, it can also be easily used by individuals. You obviously won't be able to do the group activities suggested, but you can consider how you would answer the questions and write your thoughts in the space provided.

▶ You may find it helpful to talk to a prayer partner about what you have learnt, and ask them to pray for you as you try and apply what you are learning to your life.

▶ The New International Version of the text is printed in the book. If you use a different version, then read from your own Bible as well.

INTRODUCTION

Have you ever read the back pages of a novel first? Have you ever been so desperate to see how the plot unravels that you've sneaked a peek at the final scene?

As Christians, we already know the final scene in God's Big Story. We know that Jesus will return again to wrap up the world and take us home to heaven. What we need to do is look back over God's story so that we know why the last scene is so breathtaking and exciting. We need to trace God's Big Story through the Bible, so that we can rediscover our heritage, our future, and our part in God's plan.

From before the beginning of time, God's desire was for a people who belonged to him, a people marked by holiness; a true community which would transform society as they lived by his radical values. Adam and Eve were the first to enjoy this intimacy with God but paradise ended when sin crept in. People's sinfulness has separated them from God ever since. And the rest of the Bible's story recounts how God has taken the initiative to restore that broken relationship and to recover community.

In Old Testament times the the blood of animal sacrifices symbolically cleansed the people's sins so they could approach God. In the New Testament, Jesus' death paid the price for sin once and for all. Sin no longer needs to be a barrier between us and a holy God. All those who believe in Jesus, who turn their backs on sin and turn their faces towards God in repentance, become part of that new humanity, part of the kingdom of God, part of the people God has been drawing to himself throughout history, a people he is still calling.

God's story is reaching its climax and the final scene has already been written. Today God's people, called the church, still have a central role in God's Big Story. We are called to live and speak out the gospel, to guard God's truth and live like Jesus. Church is not something we can opt in or opt out of. It is central to God's plan for humanity, it is the display of his wisdom to the world, and it is the context where we can learn who God called us to be and how he wants us to live. Church is where we can be part of the greatest story ever told. Let's learn how to give our best for God's greatest idea – the church.

CALLED TO COMMUNITY

 Aim: To become the true community that God intended church to be

Do you remember the children's chorus *Jesus bids us shine with a pure, clear light*? It refers to us being in our small corners, and perhaps we have taken this far too literally. We have privatised our faith and forgotten that God calls us to be a community of people who will love him and whose unity will demonstrate to heaven and earth that his idea of church is good.

TO SET THE SCENE

When you think of church, what words come to mind? Brainstorm your ideas together as a group. How would one of your non-Christian colleagues or friends describe church? What do you think God thinks of church?

READ GENESIS 1:26–28

Then God said, "Let us make man in our image, in our likeness, and let them rule over the fish of the sea and the birds of the air, over the livestock, over all the earth, and over all the creatures that move along the ground."

So God created man in his own image,
in the image of God he created him;
male and female he created them.

God blessed them and said to them, "Be fruitful and increase in number; fill the earth and subdue it. Rule over the fish of the sea and the birds of the air and over every living creature that moves on the ground."

Genesis 1:26–28

From the first pages of the Bible to the last we can trace God's plan to build a community. In Genesis, God calls Abraham to start the process of community building. Later in Exodus 6:7 he promises the beleaguered Israelites, suffering in exile, 'I will take you as my own people, and I will be your God'. And the Big Story of God's redemption plan to build not just a Jewish nation but a 'people of God' continues with individuals like Hosea, John the Baptist and Paul, charged to 'make ready a people prepared for the Lord' (Lk. 1:17). The book of Revelation ends with that dream being fulfilled as the New Jerusalem comes down out of heaven and a voice is heard saying 'They will be his people, and God himself will be with them and be their God' (Rev. 21:3).

1. What evidence is there in Genesis 1:26–28 that community was part of God's plan from the beginning?

2. What can we learn about community from how God exists in community – Father, Son and Holy Spirit?

> *As individuals we only discover the potential of our imago dei, made in the image of God, as we take our place in community; for this we have been designed by the God who is himself the triune community. There our personal uniqueness finds its God-centred context.*
>
> **Jeff Lucas[1]**

WHAT DOES **SEARCH** **THE BIBLE SAY?**

3. What kind of community does God want for the church? Look at Galatians 3:26–29, Ephesians 2:11–21, Revelation 14:6.

WHAT DOES **SEARCH** **THE BIBLE SAY?**

4. Why is striving for true community worthwhile? What are some of the results? Look at Acts 2:42–47, John 13:34–35, Ephesians 3:7–11.

5. What new insights do you gain by applying these verses to the church in the corporate sense in which they were intended?

- ❯ 1 Corinthians 3:16
- ❯ Ephesians 2:10
- ❯ Ephesians 6:10-18

HOW DOES THIS

APPLY TO ME

6. How has being part of the church community helped you grow as a Christian and discover more about yourself, your strengths and weaknesses?

7. Why are we often reluctant to develop community in church? What hinders us?

APPLY THIS TO

MY CHURCH

8. What can you do to develop the sense of community in your church and housegroup? Discuss together realistic goals you can aim for.

ENGAGING WITH

THE WORLD

9. How could recovering community within the church help to recover a sense of community in your locality? What does Christian community have to offer our world?

It is ... God's unmistakeable purpose to have a people of his own, and by his amazing grace it is the utterly undeserved privilege of all who belong to Christ to belong to this community, the people of God.

Alan Stibbs[2]

WORSHIP

Adoration – Begin by praising God for his glorious plans for the church. Use some of the Bible verses given in question 3 and 4 to help focus your prayers.

Confession – Ask for God's forgiveness for the times we have failed to act as community: when our gossip has hurt fellow believers, when we have failed to support those in need, when we have not loved others as Christ would have done.

Thanksgiving – Thank God for the specific examples of fellowship and community you have experienced in church life.

Supplication – Spend time praying for each other and the needs of the group.

BOOKS TO READ

The Fellowship of the King by Liam Goligher[3] explores the vision of fellowship and community presented in the Bible, as well as highlighting the urgent need for community in contemporary society. He explains how meeting, encouraging and growing together as Christians actually achieves community, purpose and ultimately fellowship with the king.

Messy Church by Lucy Moore[4] gives creative ideas for drawing your church community together for fun, food, fellowship and worship.

FOR NEXT WEEK

Take steps to be an active part of the Christian community:

▶ Ask God to show you your particular role in the church community.

▶ Meet up with another member of your church/housegroup and pray together.

▶ Look out for a Christian who is in need and do something practical to help them.

▶ Make a phone call or write a letter/email to encourage another Christian.

CHOSEN BY GOD

Aim: To recognise God has chosen us to bring hope to the world

Most of us have memories of being in the playground and shouting 'Pick me, pick me', wanting to be chosen for the sports team or make it in the 'in' crowd. That desire to be chosen, to be valued, resurfaces many times in adulthood – when we're looking for a promotion or marriage partner, when we want God to use us in a particular ministry or to answer our prayers. The truth is that God has already picked us, he has chosen the church to be his precious possession. But we weren't the first to be chosen. God started his community building by calling Abraham to be the father of the nation of Israel. Yet from the earliest days God had in mind a much bigger picture, a much wider vision. He wanted to gather a people from all nations who would bring hope to the world.

TO SET THE SCENE

Share with the group an occasion when you wanted to be chosen for something. Explain what happened and what you learnt from the experience.

READ 1 PETER 2:9–12

But you are a chosen people, a royal priesthood, a holy nation, a people belonging to God, that you may declare the praises of him who called you out of darkness into his wonderful light. Once you were not a people, but now you are the people of God; once you had not received mercy, but now you have received mercy.

Dear friends, I urge you, as aliens and strangers in the world, to abstain from sinful desires, which war against your soul. Live such good lives among the pagans that, though they accuse you of doing wrong, they may see your good deeds and glorify God on the day he visits us.

1 Peter 2:9–12

1. Put these verses into your own words. Brainstorm your ideas on each phrase until you come up with a version of the passage the whole group agrees on.

2. According to these verses what has God chosen us for? What has he chosen us to do?

ENGAGING WITH

THE WORLD

3. Being chosen by God isn't an excuse for arrogance or immorality. What can we learn from these verses about how to relate to:

▶ Work colleagues of other faiths
▶ The other parents at the school gate
▶ Unbelieving family members
▶ Friends who aren't Christians

> *God called and chose Israel, not at the expense of the rest, but for the sake of the rest.*
> ### *Chris Wright[5]*

The Israelites were supposed to be the gateway to God's plan for a worldwide community of faith, living evidence of the type of relationship that God offered to all who would trust him. But Israel failed to keep her covenant with God or to share his love with others and today the nation is still reeling from its disobedience. Some theologians believe she has forfeited her place and the church is the new Israel and the recipient of all God's blessings. Others believe there is still a future for the nation distinct from the church. Whatever your view, we can agree that both Israel and the church were chosen by God to bring living hope to a dying world.

WHAT DOES SEARCH THE BIBLE SAY?

4. Israel too was chosen by God. Look at the following verses and find some of the parallels between the church and Israel.

	Israel	The church
Same role:	Exodus 19:3–6	1 Peter 2:9
	Genesis 12:3	Matthew 28:16–20
Same value to God:	Hosea 2:16,19–20	Ephesians 5:25–27
	Deuteronomy 7:6	Titus 2:14
Same criteria for belonging to God:		
	Deuteronomy 10:16; 30:6	Romans 2:28–29

HOW DOES THIS APPLY TO ME

5. Like Israel, the church is called to be distinct from the surrounding culture. What did that mean for Israel? What do you think it means for us today?

As church, our holy lives, message of truth and compassionate love are meant to offer hope to the world, a promise that there is more to life, and that change is possible. This is not a pipe-dream or naive optimism, it can be a reality. But if the church is going to fulfil its calling, it needs to recover its firm conviction that the gospel is life-changing, Jesus' truth is worth believing and the Holy Spirit is more powerful than we've yet experienced.

APPLY THIS TO MY CHURCH

6. What problems do you see within the church that prevent us bringing hope to the world?

*"I am God. I have called you to live right and well.
I have taken responsibility for you, kept you safe.
I have set you among my people to bind them to me,
and provided you as a lighthouse to the nations,
To make a start at bringing people into the open, into light:
opening blind eyes,
releasing prisoners from dungeons,
emptying the dark prisons.
I am God.*

Isaiah 42:5–8 (The Message)

SESSION 2

7. In what particular ways do people need hope in your community?

8. How could your church demonstrate that Christ meets these deep needs? How could you be a 'lighthouse' in your locality?

WORSHIP

When he thought about being chosen by God, the apostle Paul's response was worship.

> Oh, the depth of the riches of the wisdom and knowledge of God!
> How unsearchable his judgments, and his paths beyond tracing out!
> "Who has known the mind of the Lord? Or who has been his counsellor?"
> "Who has ever given to God, that God should repay him?"
> For from him and through him and to him are all things.
> To him be the glory forever! Amen.

Romans 11:33-36

Spend time thanking God for desiring us, for making us his people, his bride, his royal priesthood, his holy nation. Pray through some of the Scriptures quoted above, such as 1 Peter 2:9-11. Then pray about how your church could be a lighthouse and ask God whether he wants you to make any of your ideas for question 8 into reality. Pray through the specific ministries your church is already engaged in and ask for his wisdom and guidance as you try to bring hope to your community.

FURTHER STUDY

Isaiah 60 describes Israel as the catalyst for the hope of all nations being brought under God's reign in the New Jerusalem. Study and meditate on this passage with the help of a few commentaries.

FOR NEXT WEEK

Jesus was the ultimate One chosen by God to bring hope to the world. Read through one of the gospels reflecting on Jesus' attitude, actions and focus as he did God's work. What lessons can you learn from his example?

LIVING OUT HOLINESS

Aim: To reflect on God's holiness of God and his call for us to live holy lives

Contemporary and relevant are the watch words of the church today. We want to attract people into the church and make them feel comfortable. All this is good, but in striving to make church accessible we often fall into the trap of presenting a tame, manageable god, a god bereft of his transcendence, his holiness and his otherness – the very things people are searching for. When we remove God's holiness, we not only remove the essence of who he is but the essence of who we are and what we are called to become.

TO SET THE SCENE

What makes the church distinct from any other club or organisation people may belong to? What can the church offer people that they can't get from any other group – the unique characteristics of church?

READ EXODUS 32:1–6

When the people saw that Moses was so long in coming down from the mountain, they gathered around Aaron and said, "Come, make us gods who will go before us. As for this fellow Moses who brought us up out of Egypt, we don't know what has happened to him."

Aaron answered them, "Take off the gold ear-rings that your wives, your sons and your daughters are wearing, and bring them to me." So all the people took off their ear-rings and brought them to Aaron. He took what they handed him and made it into an idol cast in the shape of a calf, fashioning it with a tool. Then they said, "These are your gods, O Israel, who brought you up out of Egypt."

When Aaron saw this, he built an altar in front of the calf and announced, "Tomorrow there will be a festival to the Lᴏʀᴅ." So the next day the people rose early and sacrificed burnt offerings and presented fellowship offerings. Afterward they sat down to eat and drink and got up to indulge in revelry.

Exodus 32:1–6

1. Why did the Israelites make a golden calf?

2. What did they like so much about this hand-made god?

Donald McCullough in *The Trivialization of God*[6] suggests that the church is in danger of revising God to make him a god we can manage or fully understand. He outlines four possible 'golden calf' gods we may make:

The God of **my cause** – we begin with an idea and make Scripture, and therefore God, endorse our thinking

The God of **my understanding** – we see our views as orthodox and everyone who disagrees with us is in error

The God of **my experience** – we make our own experience of God define spirituality and all other experiences of God must mirror ours

The God of **my comfort** – God's role is to satisfy me and make me happy

APPLY THIS TO

MY CHURCH

3. Which of the 'golden calf' gods do you think we in the British church are most likely to make?

4. If we edit God's holiness, what kind of god are we left with?

> *I cannot completely believe in a God that I can understand completely.*
>
> **Loralee Hagan**[7]

5. What steps can we take to become more aware of God's holiness and transcendence in our churches?

Reverence and awe have often been replaced by a yawn of familiarity. The consuming fire has been domesticated into a candle flame, adding a bit of religious atmosphere, perhaps, but no heat, no blinding light, no power for purification.

Donald McCullough[8]

Personal holiness is a complete, and at the same time, ongoing process.

6. In what sense have we already been made holy? Look at 1 Corinthians 1:2, 6:9–11, Hebrews 10:10.

7. In what sense is holiness an ongoing process? Look at John 17:17, 2 Corinthians 7:1.

Holiness is really a dynamic attitude of wholehearted availability to the purposes of our dynamic God.

Jeff Lucas[9]

8. What do the prophets and historical books of the Bible teach us about what holiness looks like in practice?

- ▶ 1 Kings 18:16–46
- ▶ Isaiah 1:10–17
- ▶ Isaiah 58
- ▶ Micah 6:8

9. What practices or circumstances helped the Israelites grow in holiness?

10. What measures can we take to grow in holiness?

HOLINESS IN ACTION

> *He has showed you, O man, what is good. And what does the LORD require of you? To act justly and to love mercy and to walk humbly with your God.*
>
> **Micah 6:8**

The Old Testament prophets taught the Israelites that holiness was not a private affair – it had to make a difference to the social and moral ethics of the community. Jesus and the New Testament writers repeat the same message to us.

Take a look at the following three issues. How will you respond?

1   Climate Change

The world's poorest countries feel the greatest impact of climate change. The World Health Organisation reports that each year 150,000 die as a result of climate change.

What can you do?
- Find out how you can cut carbon emissions
- Take action and make changes where you can
- Put pressure on local and national government
- Contact Tearfund for more information (www.tearfund.org)

2   Regeneration of Communities

Existing schemes and agencies can no longer cope with the ever-increasing needs of local communities and the door is wide open for those willing to be involved in regeneration, engage with local government and serve their area.

What can you do?
- Speak to local agencies about where your church can get involved
- Support an ongoing project or start a new one
- Contact Faithworks for resources and training (www.faithworks.info)

3   People trafficking

Two hundred years after transatlantic slavery was abolished, people trafficking is still a huge issue. Conservative figures estimate 1.2 million children are trafficked each year and between 142 and 1,420 women are trafficked into and within the UK for sexual exploitation each year.

What can you do?
- Put pressure on national government, the European Union, via your Euro MP, and the United Nations
- Contact Stop The Traffik (www.stopthetraffik.org) for information on how you can raise awareness of the issue, pray, and support projects such as safe houses.

WORSHIP

Choose some songs or hymns on the theme of God's holiness. Then spend time meditating and praying through Isaiah 6:1–8. Focus on:

▶ God's holiness (v1–4)

▶ Our sinfulness (v5)

▶ Our forgiveness through Christ's death on the cross (v6–7)

▶ Our ability now to approach God and to be used in his service (v8)

Pray through your work/family situations and spheres of influence and say again to God 'Here I am. Send me.' Pray that as you become more like Jesus and grow in holiness, your testimony would attract others to Christ.

BOOKS TO READ

The Trivialization of God by Donald McCullough and Jeremy McQuoid's *How to set your heart on fire.*[10]

FOR NEXT WEEK

Ask God how he wants you to grow in holiness this week:

▶ Is there a command he wants you to obey?

▶ Is there a sin you need to repent of?

▶ Are there priorities you need to rearrange so that you can have a daily devotional time?

▶ Is there a trial or suffering he wants you to learn obedience through?

▶ Is there an issue of justice God wants you to fight for?

▶ Is there someone in need or suffering that God wants you to serve?

▶ Is there an area of your life where outward piety needs to be matched by a devoted heart?

BOUNDARIES AND MARGINS

Aim: To mirror Jesus' inclusivity

Whether it is in parenting, work, the type of holidays we enjoy or even evangelism, we all have boundaries. Boundaries demarcate our comfort zone and we rarely stray beyond them. Some boundaries are good and protective but all are worth analysing. The new community created by Jesus' death crosses every human boundary and barrier to include people from everywhere. And he challenges us to examine our personal barriers and welcome all into his kingdom of grace. He urges us to act like a worldwide family rather than mirror the fragmentation of our culture.

TO SET THE SCENE

Discuss together the profile of your church. What is the general age, social class, ethnic background, gender of the congregation? To what extent do you reflect the make-up of the community around you? Are there some groups of people who may feel unwelcome in your church?

READ JOHN 4:4-26

Now he had to go through Samaria. So he came to a town in Samaria called Sychar, near the plot of ground Jacob had given to his son Joseph. Jacob's well was there, and Jesus, tired as he was from the journey, sat down by the well. It was about the sixth hour.

When a Samaritan woman came to draw water, Jesus said to her, "Will you give me a drink?" (His disciples had gone into the town to buy food.)

The Samaritan woman said to him, "You are a Jew and I am a Samaritan woman. How can you ask me for a drink?" (For Jews do not associate with Samaritans.)

Jesus answered her, "If you knew the gift of God and who it is that asks you for a drink, you would have asked him and he would have given you living water."

"Sir," the woman said, "you have nothing to draw with and the well is deep.

Where can you get this living water? Are you greater than our father Jacob, who gave us the well and drank from it himself, as did also his sons and his flocks and herds?"

Jesus answered, "Everyone who drinks this water will be thirsty again, but whoever drinks the water I give him will never thirst. Indeed, the water I give him will become in him a spring of water welling up to eternal life."

The woman said to him, "Sir, give me this water so that I won't get thirsty and have to keep coming here to draw water."

He told her, "Go, call your husband and come back."

"I have no husband," she replied.

Jesus said to her, "You are right when you say you have no husband. The fact is, you have had five husbands, and the man you now have is not your husband. What you have just said is quite true."

"Sir," the woman said, "I can see that you are a prophet. Our fathers worshipped on this mountain, but you Jews claim that the place where we must worship is in Jerusalem."

Jesus declared, "Believe me, woman, a time is coming when you will worship the Father neither on this mountain nor in Jerusalem. You Samaritans worship what you do not know; we worship what we do know, for salvation is from the Jews. Yet a time is coming and has now come when the true worshippers will worship the Father in spirit and truth, for they are the kind of worshippers the Father seeks. God is spirit, and his worshippers must worship in spirit and in truth."

The woman said, "I know that Messiah" (called Christ) "is coming. When he comes, he will explain everything to us."

Then Jesus declared, "I who speak to you am he."

John 4:4-26

1. The woman said to Jesus 'How can you ask me for a drink?' Why was it so culturally taboo for Jesus to have this conversation?

He touched untouchables with love and washed the guilty clean.
Communion Service, Common Worship

WHAT DOES
SEARCH
THE BIBLE SAY?

2. Jesus welcomed those considered outsiders in the Jewish culture to be insiders in his kingdom. Look at some examples:

▶ Matthew 8:5–13
▶ Mark 1:40–42
▶ Mark 2:13–14
▶ Mark 5:1–20

In Near Eastern thinking, sitting at a table with someone was considered an act of intimacy and fellowship. To offer hospitality was to give honour and trusting acceptance. Refusal to share a meal conversely signalled rejection and disapproval. Jesus took the everyday practice of sharing a meal and made it a living parable.
Jeff Lucas[11]

WHAT DOES
SEARCH
THE BIBLE SAY?

3. How did Jesus respond to those who criticised his choice of dinner guests?

▶ Mark 2:15–17
▶ Luke 7:31–35
▶ Luke 15:1–7
▶ Luke 19:7–10

HOW DOES THIS
?
APPLY TO ME

4. At your stage of life what is the equivalent of 'table fellowship'? In what practical ways do you develop relationships with non-Christians?

5. We often face dilemmas when we imitate Jesus' wide open approach to evangelism. What would you say to:

▶ A student wondering what clubs and societies to join at university in order to have witnessing opportunities.

▶ A young mum who has joined book clubs and been out socially with the other mothers from her child's school. She has tried to develop friendships but knows sooner or later a clash of values is going to make relationships awkward.

▶ A business man who knows that if he socialises with his clients, his church friends will assume he has compromised his faith.

6. Jesus did not just draw outsiders in, he invited those on the margins of the faith community, such as women and children, to take centre stage. Which groups do you think are marginalised within the church today?

7. How could your church shows it values these groups? What practical ideas could you implement?

One of the ways we can show we value children is to share the gospel with them. The Christian researcher George Barna believes that children are more open and receptive to the gospel that at any other time in their lives. He says "The data shows that churches can have a very significant impact on the worldview of people, but they must start with an intentional process introduced to people at a very young age. Waiting until someone is in their teens or young adult years misses the window of opportunity."[12] And in Israel, the responsibility to pass on the Big Story to the next generation was given to parents, not to the priests.

8. How can we best present the gospel to children? What bad practices do we need to avoid? What are the different stages of their development and what is relevant at which stage?

9. Sum up this session together. How can we mirror Jesus' inclusivity in our churches? Think through:

▶ How can you transform church from feeling like a random selection of interest groups into an inclusive community?

▶ Are there measures could you take to make those who are outsiders in society feel welcome in your church?

▶ Are there other churches in your community you should be working with rather than against?

▶ Are there individuals in your church you need to embrace rather than reject?

WORSHIP

Once we were 'separate from Christ, excluded ... without hope and without God in the world. But now in Christ Jesus we who were once far away have been brought near through the blood of Christ' (Eph. 2:12–13). Thank God for that! We were once outsiders, excluded from the community of faith. For us to become the people of God meant Jesus took the punishment our sins deserved. He was marginalised, excluded and ill-treated in our place.

Meditate together on the cost of our salvation.

He was despised and rejected by men,
a man of sorrows, and familiar with suffering.
Like one from whom men hide their faces
he was despised, and we esteemed him not.

Surely he took up our infirmities
and carried our sorrows,
yet we considered him stricken by God,
smitten by him, and afflicted.

But he was pierced for our transgressions,
he was crushed for our iniquities;
the punishment that brought us peace was upon him,
and by his wounds we are healed.

We all, like sheep, have gone astray,
each of us has turned to his own way;
and the LORD has laid on him
the iniquity of us all.

He was oppressed and afflicted,
yet he did not open his mouth;
he was led like a lamb to the slaughter,
and as a sheep before her shearers is silent,
so he did not open his mouth.

By oppression and judgment he was taken away.
And who can speak of his descendants?
For he was cut off from the land of the living;
for the transgression of my people he was stricken.

He was assigned a grave with the wicked,
and with the rich in his death,
though he had done no violence,
nor was any deceit in his mouth.

Yet it was the LORD's will to crush him and cause him to suffer,
and though the LORD makes his life a guilt offering,
he will see his offspring and prolong his days,
and the will of the LORD will prosper in his hand.

Isaiah 53:3–10

Being grateful for our salvation is only part of the process. We need to ask for God's help to love others as Christ did, to reach out to those on the margins of our church and society. Use Jeff Lucas' words to help focus your prayers.

We give thanks to you, Father of
the One Family of God.

Once we were dead, but now have been made
alive with Christ, your new creation people.

Once we were outcasts, but now we
sit at the top table of your grace.

Once we were alone, but we have come in
from the cold, to sit at the fireside of your
love; joined with you, and joined together.

Through us, may love's call reach those
still frozen in fear, and draw them in.

Through us, may unity and mercy be
modelled, a winsome demonstration of
how life was meant to be.

Help us to truly honour each other.

Help us celebrate our differences, and not
fear them or be threatened by them.

Help us gather around what we truly share.

*Strengthen those who suffer simply because they love
your name; bring comfort, hope, justice, and freedom.*

In the Name of Christ we pray.

Amen

BOOKS TO READ

Just Walk Across the Room: Simple Steps Pointing People to Faith[13] by Bill Hybels:
this book encourages us to get out of our comfort zones, break down the barriers
and begin connecting with people.

Everyone's Normal Until You get to Know Them[14] by John Ortberg challenges us to
develop relationships with imperfect people (like ourselves) and discover the rich-
ness of community.

FOR NEXT WEEK
Watch out for opportunities to mirror Jesus' inclusivity. For example:

- ❯ Don't just speak to those in your usual clique after church, speak to someone different.

- ❯ Invite a newcomer back for Sunday lunch.

- ❯ Invest time in getting to know one of your work colleagues.

KINGDOM PEOPLE

Aim: To understand what the kingdom of God is and our role in it

When was the last time you heard a sermon on the kingdom of God? In fact, when was the last time you even thought about the kingdom of God? We often think of Jesus as our king but rarely of him having a kingdom. And yet Jesus' sermons were always about the kingdom. He wanted people to know that God's rule – his values, his truth and justice – had broken into our world at his first coming and would be fully consummated on his return. The Jews had expected the kingdom to be geographical and political. But Jesus turned their thinking upside down – he came in peace not war, he was crowned on a cross not a throne, and he brought a whole new set of values which would define his kingdom people.

TO SET THE SCENE

Consider your role as a citizen of the United Kingdom:

▶ What are the defining characteristics of this kingdom?

▶ What do you think are the key values of this kingdom?

▶ To what extent do you feel allegiance to this kingdom?

READ MATTHEW 4:23, 6:9–10, 13:44–46, MARK 1:14–15, LUKE 17:20–21

Jesus went throughout Galilee, teaching in their synagogues, preaching the good news of the kingdom, and healing every disease and sickness among the people.

Matthew 4:23

This, then, is how you should pray: Our Father in heaven, hallowed be your name, your kingdom come, your will be done on earth as it is in heaven.

Matthew 6:9–10

The kingdom of heaven is like treasure hidden in a field. When a man found it, he hid it again, and then in his joy went and sold all he had and bought that field.

Again, the kingdom of heaven is like a merchant looking for fine pearls. When he found one of great value, he went away and sold everything he had and bought it.

Matthew 13:44–46

After John was put in prison, Jesus went into Galilee, proclaiming the good news of God. "The time has come," he said. "The kingdom of God is near. Repent and believe the good news!"

Mark 1:14–15

Once, having been asked by the Pharisees when the kingdom of God would come, Jesus replied, "The kingdom of God does not come with your careful observation, nor will people say, 'Here it is,' or 'There it is,' because the kingdom of God is within you.

Luke 17:20–21

1. What does the term 'kingdom of God' mean? What do these verses teach us?

WHAT DOES
SEARCH
THE BIBLE SAY?

2. How did Jesus signal that the kingdom was coming and he was the king? Look at Zechariah 9:9 and Matthew 21:1–11.

3. How would you explain the kingdom of God to a new Christian? What modern day analogies could you use?

4. Brainstorm together a charter for the values that define Jesus' kingdom.

ENGAGING WITH
THE WORLD

5. Evidence of God's kingdom is found in the most surprising places when people, not necessarily Christians, imitate him and live by his values. Where have you seen the kingdom of God breaking into your world? Where have you seen his rule being established?

All too often in Western society, people respond to the message of the evangelist by adding a new compartment to their life.

Roy McCloughry[15]

To step into the kingdom is to surrender to Christ every right.

Jeff Lucas[16]

6. Being citizens of the kingdom of God means we owe total allegiance to him. What else contends for our loyalty today?

7. What practical measures can we take to stay faithful to God and his kingdom values?

8. How can we as church demonstrate to the world that the kingdom of God is here?

9. How does the truth that the kingdom of God will one day come in all its fullness help us deal with:

- ▶ Suffering
- ▶ Ridicule
- ▶ Sacrifice
- ▶ Bereavement

It's Sunday, but Monday's coming

The message of the kingdom calls us to live all of life under God, and for God, and so the teaching of the church must equip us for every day of life – for Mondays as well as Sundays.

Consider following the example of Brookside Church in Reading. They changed the format of their business meeting to focus on what members were doing outside of church rather than inside it. The had a 'business of the people of the church' meeting instead!

You could do the same in your church. If you have space, give each person a stall so estate agents, policemen and women, teachers, physiotherapists and care workers can display information and be available to talk about what they do for most of their lives. At the end of the evening have a prayer time. Pray for the people who have talked about their jobs and for the particular issues they face at work.

You could also have a 'business of the people of the church' meeting focusing on what people do in their leisure time. Invite some of the congregation to talk about their roles as school governors, Girl Guide and Boy Scout leaders, members of Rotary clubs and football teams. Again pray for each other and the various ways your church is having an influence in the community.

As a regular way of connecting Sunday morning with Monday morning you could have a 3T (this time tomorrow) spot in each Sunday morning service. Invite a member of the congregation to share what they will be doing at work on Monday morning and then pray for them.

For more resources about Christianity in the workplace visit www.worknet.org or www.licc.org.uk

WORSHIP

But seek first his kingdom and his righteousness...

Matthew 6:33

In silence, ask yourself if you are truly seeking God's kingdom. Are there any areas of your life which you are not submitting to his control or any situations or circumstances in which you are not obeying his rule? If it helps, write down your response on a piece of paper. Also write down what you need to do to demonstrate submissiveness to Christ.

Jesus asked us to pray that his kingdom would come. Pray together that God's rule would be established in:

▶ International conflicts
▶ National government
▶ Local institutions such as schools and universities
▶ Our church
▶ Our homes

BOOKS TO READ

If you want to look at the theme of the kingdom of God throughout Scripture, try *God's Big Picture: Tracing the Storyline of the Bible*[17] by Vaughan Roberts, and *The Goldsworthy Trilogy*[18] by Graeme Goldsworthy.

FOR NEXT WEEK

The kingdom of God is often described in terms of celebration – a lavish feast, a party after a lost coin is found. Find ways to include more celebration in your life. Take some time out to celebrate nature, a birthday or anniversary. Mark good news in your home group with a meal or organise a church party just to celebrate everything God has done for us.

TRAVELLING LIGHT

Aim: To recognise that disciple-makers never cease to be disciples

People often say 'It's the journey, not the destination, that counts.' But for the Christian both are important. From the call to Abram to "Leave your country, your people and your father's household and go to the land that I will show you" (Gen. 12:1), God's people have always been on the move because God is on the move. His gospel is growing and expanding, reaching new places and deepening in people's hearts. And God invites flawed, broken people to be part of his plans, to go on their own journey of faith, growing in holiness and spiritual maturity as they fulfil their task of the great commission. God provides signposts and a roadmap to help us on this kingdom trek but all the while we need to keep our focus on the destination. Our journey's end is heaven.

TO SET THE SCENE
Invite members of the group to present a 'spiritual life map', sharing something of their spiritual journey so far. It could be how they became a Christian or what God has been doing in their life more recently.

READ MARK 1:2–4; JOHN 3:16–17, 16:7; LUKE 11:49; MATTHEW 9:37–38

It is written in Isaiah the prophet:

> *"I will send my messenger ahead of you,*
> *who will prepare your way"—*
> *"a voice of one calling in the desert,*
> *'Prepare the way for the Lord,*
> *make straight paths for him.' "*

And so John came, baptising in the desert region and preaching a baptism of repentance for the forgiveness of sins.

Mark 1:2–4

"For God so loved the world that he gave his one and only Son, that whoever believes in him shall not perish but have eternal life. For God did not send his Son into the world to condemn the world, but to save the world through him.

John 3:16–17

But I tell you the truth: It is for your good that I am going away. Unless I go away, the Counsellor will not come to you; but if I go, I will send him to you.

John 16:7

Because of this, God in his wisdom said, 'I will send them prophets and apostles, some of whom they will kill and others they will persecute.'

Luke 11:49

Then he said to his disciples, "The harvest is plentiful but the workers are few. Ask the Lord of the harvest, therefore, to send out workers into his harvest field."

Matthew 9:37–38

1. What is the evidence that God sends people out to fulfil his salvation plan?

 2. Rewrite Matthew 28:18–20 in your own words. What does Jesus send us out to do, what is our commission?

 3. How do we make disciples? What is the church's role and responsibility?

 4. Look at the following passages. What evidence is there that the first disciple-makers never ceased to be disciples, that they, like us, were flawed?

▶ Acts 15:36–41

▶ Galatians 2:11–13

 5. What would you say to someone who felt they were too broken and had too much baggage for God to send them out into service?

God knows that weak disciples need signposts and landmarks to help them persevere on the journey of faith, to remind them they are part of God's story, and that their destination is in sight. God chose baptism and communion to be solid, tangible, living symbols to help us reflect on the salvation story so far and our part in it.

> *Baptism and Eucharist are mini-dramas of salvation using material props – water, bread and wine. By washing a new believer, and by eating and drinking together, Christians use their bodies to re-enact the story of God's gracious salvation in Christ. Through seeing, moving, touching, tasting, and smelling, God speaks again the creative and redeeming Word.*
>
> **Donald McCullough[19]**

6. What does communion represent? What is the symbolism behind this sacrament? Look at Exodus 12:1–13, 21–28; 1 Corinthians 11:23–26.

WHAT DOES
SEARCH
THE BIBLE SAY?

7. What does the sacrament of baptism mean? How does it remind us that our salvation and discipleship is costly? Look at Romans 6:3–4.

8. How do the sacraments of communion and baptism help us on our spiritual journey?

> *The sacraments were intended to establish, strengthen and distinguish the church and to equip her for kingdom life and mission in every age and context.*
>
> **T.M. Moore[20]**

HOW DOES THIS
?
APPLY TO ME

9. What else has helped you grow as a Christian? What have been the key factors in your own discipleship journey?

10. As you reflect on your own spiritual journey, share where you think God is sending you. What people, circumstances or situation is he sending you into, to live and speak out his gospel?

WORSHIP

Some church traditions use liturgy to declare their faith and help keep people spiritually on track. Speak this creed aloud together to affirm your allegiance to Christ.

> *I believe in the one true God, the Father, the Almighty, and his only begotten Son, Jesus Christ our Lord and Saviour with his Holy Spirit, the giver of life to everything, three in one substance, one divinity, one lordship, one kingdom, one faith, one baptism, in the holy catholic apostolic church, which lives forever. Amen.*

The Apostolic Tradition (21.12)[21]

If it is appropriate, share communion together. Then, in twos, pray through people's responses to question 10.

BOOKS TO READ

The Master Plan of Evangelism[22] and *The Master Plan of Discipleship*[23] by Robert Coleman or *The life you've always wanted* by John Ortberg.[24]

FOR NEXT WEEK

Where are you on your spiritual journey? Are you still walking with a spring in your step, has a rough road caused you to slow down or do you feel like you have dropped out of the race? Spend time this week taking stock of your own spiritual life and consider what measures you need to take to keep growing as a Christian and finish the journey well. Use the material below to help you.

Signs of Grace

The mission of God and the people of God are always on the move. God has given us signposts and a road map to help us navigate our journey but sometimes we need to make our own markers.

As Abram journeyed and saw God unfolding his salvation plan and keeping his promises, he built altars. This was a practical demonstration commemorating God's work, celebrating his faithfulness and underlining Abram's dependence on him.

> So Abram left, as the Lord had told him … and they set out for the land of Canaan, and they arrived there. Abram travelled through the land as far as the site of the great tree of Moreh at Shechem. At that time the Canaanites were in the land. The Lord appeared to Abram and said, "To your offspring I will give this land." So he built an altar there to the Lord, who had appeared to him. From there he went on toward the hills east of Bethel and pitched his tent, with Bethel on the west and Ai on the east. There he built an altar to the Lord and called on the name of the Lord. Then Abram set out and continued toward the Negev.
>
> **Genesis 12:4–9**

Think about ways you could mark significant milestones on your spiritual journey – ways you could express your gratitude to God, testify to his grace and deepen your own faith.

Below are some suggestions:

- You could show your gratitude by giving back some of the financial resources God has blessed you with. Make a generous gift to a church ministry, mission situation or individual.
- Record God's faithfulness on paper. Try keeping a journal where you note down what God is teaching you at significant times or turning points in your spiritual life. Perhaps write a thank you letter to God which you can reread when you are struggling with issues or doubting your faith.
- Plant a tree or flower to record particular times of blessing, a time when you met with God in a special way or when he answered your prayers.
- Go on a foreign missions trip or get involved in a new ministry, something which will stretch your faith and demonstrate to God your complete dependence on him.
- Take a photo. Whenever God reminds you he is working in you and through you – an evangelistic conversation with a colleague, knowing God's strength when you needed it most, an answer to prayer about your children, a breakthrough in your ministry – take a photo. Collate them into a special album and note down why you took a picture that day.

LEADERS' GUIDE

TO HELP YOU LEAD

You may have led a housegroup many times before or this may be your first time. Here is some advice on how to lead these studies:

▶ As a group leader, you don't have to be an expert or a lecturer. You are there to facilitate the learning of the group members – helping them to discover for themselves the wisdom in God's word. You should not be doing most of the talking or dishing out the answers, whatever the group expects from you.

▶ You do need to be aware of the group's dynamics, however. People can be quite quick to label themselves and each other in a group situation. One person might be seen as the expert, another the moaner who always has something to complain about. One person may be labelled as quiet and not be expected to contribute; another person may always jump in with something to say. Be aware of the different type of individuals in the group, but don't allow the labels to stick. You may need to encourage those who find it hard to get a word in, and quieten down those who always have something to say. Talk to members between sessions to find out how they feel about the group.

▶ The sessions are planned to engage every member in active learning. Of course you cannot force anyone to take part if they don't want to, but it won't be too easy to be a spectator. Activities that ask everyone to write down a word, or talk in twos, and then report back to the group are there for a reason. They give everyone space to think and form their opinion, even if not everyone voices it out loud.

▶ Do adapt the sessions for your group as you feel is appropriate. Some groups may know each other very well and be prepared to talk at a deep level. New groups may take a bit of time to get to know each other before making themselves vulnerable, but encourage members to share their lives with each other.

▶ You probably won't be able to tackle all the questions in each session so decide in advance which ones are most appropriate to your group and situation.

▶ Encourage a number of replies to each question. The study is not about finding a single right answer, but about sharing experiences and thoughts in order to find out how to apply the Bible to people's lives. When brainstorming, don't be too quick to evaluate the contributions. Write everything down and then have a look to see which suggestions are worth keeping.

▶ Similarly, encourage everyone to ask questions, voice doubts and discuss difficulties. Some parts of the Bible are difficult to understand. Sometimes the Christian faith throws up paradoxes. Painful things happen to us that make it difficult to see what God is doing. A housegroup should be a safe place to express all of this. If discussion doesn't resolve the issue, send everyone away to pray about it between sessions and ask your minister for advice.

▶ Give yourself time in the week to read through the Bible passage and the questions. Read the Leaders' notes for the session, as different ways of presenting the questions are sometimes suggested. However during the session don't be too quick to come in with the answer – sometimes people need space to think.

▶ Delegate as much as you like. The easiest activities to delegate are reading the text and the worship sessions, but there are other ways to involve the group members. Giving people responsibility can help them own the session much more.

▶ Pray for group members by name, that God would meet with them during the week. Pray for the group session, for a constructive and helpful time. Ask the Lord to equip you as you lead the group.

THE STRUCTURE OF EACH SESSION

Feedback: find out what people remember from the previous session, or if they have been able to act during the week on what was discussed last time.

To set the scene: an activity or a question to get everyone thinking about the subject to be studied.

Bible reading: it's important to actually read the passage you are studying during the session. Ask someone to prepare this in advance or go around the group reading a verse or two each. Don't assume everyone will be happy to read out loud.

Questions and activities: adapt these as appropriate to your group. Some groups may enjoy a more activity-based approach; some may prefer just to discuss the questions. Try out some new things!

Worship: suggestions for creative worship and prayer are included, which give everyone an opportunity to respond to God, largely individually. Use these alongside singing or other group expressions of worship. Add a prayer time with opportunities to pray for group members and their families and friends.

For next week: this gives a specific task to do during the week, helping people to continue to think about or apply what they have learned.

For further study: suggestions are given for those people who want to study the themes further. These could be included in the housegroup if you feel it's appropriate and if there is time.

WHAT YOU NEED

A list of materials that are needed is printed at the start of each session in the Leaders' Guide. In addition you will probably need:

Bibles: the main Bible passage is printed in the book so that all the members can work from the same version. It will be useful to have other Bibles available, or to ask everyone to bring their own, so that other passages and different translations can be referred to.

Paper and Pens: for people who need more space than is in the book.

Flip chart: it is helpful to write down people's comments during a brainstorming session, so that none of the suggestions are lost. They may not be space for a proper flip chart in the average lounge, and having one may make it feel too much like a business meeting or lecture. Try getting someone to write on a big sheet of paper on the floor or coffee table, and then stick this up on the wall with blu-tack.

GROUND RULES

How do people know what is expected of them in a housegroup situation? Is it ever discussed or do we just pick up clues for each other? You may find it helpful to discuss some ground rules for the housegroup at the start of this course, even if your group has been going a long time. This also gives you an opportunity to talk about how you, as the leader, see the group. Ask everyone to think about what they want to get out of the course. How do they want the group to work? What values do they want to be part of the group's experience; honesty, respect, confidentiality? How do they want their contributions to be treated? You could ask everyone to write down three ground rules on slips of paper and put them in a bowl. Pass the bowl around the group. Each person takes out a rule and reads it, and someone collates the list. Discuss the ground rules that have been suggested and come up with a top five. This method enables everyone to contribute fairly anonymously. Alternatively, if your group are all quite vocal, have a straight discussion about it!

ICONS

The aim of the session

Engaging with the world

Investigate what else the Bible says

How does this apply to me?

What about my church?

NB not all questions in each session are covered, some are self-explanatory

SESSION 1

MATERIALS NEEDED
Flip chart, pens and paper

CDs or tapes and a music system if you think it would be helpful for the worship session.

TO SET THE SCENE
Some members of the group may have had negative experiences of church, others may think church means the building you go to on Sunday. Non-Christian friends may associate church with bad music, cold stone buildings and people with no fashion sense. Whatever the group's response, encourage them to see that God is thrilled about church. For him, church is a community of believers in relationship with him: he belongs to them and they belong to him. In community, our faith is refined and we testify to the world about the power and wisdom of God (Eph. 3:10). Church isn't an optional extra for a Christian: being part of this new community is at the heart of our faith.

1. From Genesis 1:26–28 we learn God himself – Father, Son and Holy Spirit – exists in community – 'Let us make man in our image.' Therefore, as we are made in God's image, we too are designed to exist in community. God recognised it wasn't good for Adam to be alone, so he made Eve: right from the start there was community. And the plan was for that community to grow, for the pair to 'be fruitful'. This passage doesn't mean we all have to be married with children but merely indicates that all of us were designed with community in mind.

2. Encourage the group to think through how the Trinity works. The Son does the will of the Father and the Spirit does the work of the Son but there is mutual respect. The Father, Son, and Holy Spirit all have different roles but equal value. In the church community, we all have different roles, some will be leaders and others not, yet all must be esteemed and valued because all have equal value before God. Community doesn't mean we all think the same or do the same: it means there is unity but not uniformity.

3. Our community is based around our relationship with Christ and that transcends ethnic, social and sexual distinctions (Gal. 3:26–29). Through Christ's death we Gentiles can be part of the people of God. The criteria for all is the same – belief in Christ. Our community is a dynamic one, still growing and becoming a place where a holy God feels welcome (Eph. 2:11–22) and is an international one: the gospel is for all cultures (Rev. 14:6).

4. Community is worth striving for because it is God's desire for us, what we were designed for, and the results of community are also significant. The unity, prayers and dedication of the early church community seemed to unleash God's power in an unprecedented way and many were converted (Acts 2:42–47). Love for one another in community testifies to those outside that our faith is genuine (Jn. 13:34–35). A united church, in the Ephesians' case bringing together Jew and Gentile, demonstrates God's wisdom to the heavenly powers (Eph. 3:7–11).

5. Other verses in the Bible tell us that we as individuals are a temple where the Holy Spirit dwells but 1 Corinthians 3:16 says that, as a church together, we are a temple and that in a special sense God's Spirit dwells with us in community. This highlights the importance of meeting together as church and reminds us that corporately we can either welcome or grieve the Holy Spirit. Ephesians 2:10 – it's not just individuals who God has plans for but as a church we have a role to fulfil. Therefore each of us must play our part and recognise that though there may be characters we don't 'click' with, God thinks of us all as his works of art. Ephesians 6:10–18 – there is a corporate sense in which we put the armour of God on and we have a combined strength to resist the devil. Together we have strength as we rely on God's truth, live rightly, pray, and depend on his word.

6. Encourage people to be honest here. It is not always easy to be a part of community – we can be hurt by other Christians, let down by our leaders and feel undervalued. But community can also be a place where we learn about our spiritual gifts, receive encouragement in our faith, are mentored by an older Christian, work out what God wants us to do with our lives, learn about patience and forgiveness, see first hand the value and cost of unity, and learn what it means to truly follow Christ.

7. There are many reasons why we don't invest in community – we feel we don't have the time to develop relationships, we have been hurt in the past, we don't see the value of doing so, we understand faith as being solely about our individual relationship with Christ, there are people in church we wouldn't otherwise associate with.

8. Be realistic in your goals. Consider having a potluck lunch together as a housegroup once a month after church, praying together in prayer triplets every other week, inviting someone for a meal who is not in your usual crowd.

9. Non-Christians often remark on the love, welcome and friendship they find in church. We could take that sense of community outside the walls of the church by being involved in local events or hosting them. For example, invite the neighbourhood to a bonfire night or a New Years Eve party. Finding ways that we can serve and get involved in our community either as individuals or as a church allows people see the difference being in community with God and with other Christians makes to life.

SESSION 2

MATERIALS NEEDED

Flip chart, pens and paper

CDs or tapes and a music system if you think it would be helpful for the worship session.

TO SET THE SCENE

Give people time to share their experiences. We can learn many things from being chosen – thankfulness, the joy of answered prayer, the reality that what we hope for is not always best for us! We also learn lessons when we are not chosen – patience, God's timing, what is really important in life and what isn't. Help the group to see the importance and rediscover the joy of being chosen by God – far more important than getting promoted or being picked for the sports team.

2. Being chosen by God is not a licence for immorality or arrogance. We were chosen for a purpose. As priests, we are to intercede for people; offer spiritual sacrifices such as worship and our lives; do good to others (Heb. 13:16); reflect God's holiness to the world. As a holy nation we are to be distinct from the world, in the sense that God's priorities and values guide us. We belong to God and one of our roles is to tell others about all that God has done for us in salvation. The fact that we live different and good lives among unbelievers may influence them to repent and believe in God.

3. In some sense being chosen by God does separate us from those who are not yet Christians but it also gives us a responsibility for them. It means that we should to be praying for them, telling them the gospel straight but with a winsomeness; it means that we live by God's values, which may cause controversy; it calls for a spiritually disciplined life; it may mean being wrongfully accused; and we pray that as we live and share life with others over the long haul, we may influence them for Christ.

4. Israel and the church share the same calling to be priests and a holy nation (Ex. 19:3–6, 1 Pet. 2:9). We are also both called, not just for ourselves but for the sake of the world – Israel was to be a gateway to bring God's love to the Gentiles and the church is called to spread the gospel to all nations (Gen. 12:3, Mt. 28:16–20). We are both precious to God, described as his bride (Hos. 2:16,19–20, Eph. 5:27) and his very own people (Deut. 7:6 and Titus 2:14). For the

Israelites, physical circumcision was a sign of the covenant with God but God wanted more than that. From both Israel and the church he longed for a circumcised heart – a symbol of sacrificial obedience, a submitted will and faithfulness.

5. For Israel to be distinct from surrounding nations meant obeying God's law, rejecting other gods, not marrying foreigners, having a system of social justice which protected the poor and needy. We cannot physically separate ourselves from secular people or culture. Perhaps for us being distinct means holding God's values and pursuing his priorities even when we face opposition or temptation.

SESSION 3

MATERIALS NEEDED

Flip chart, pens and paper

CDs or tapes and a music system if you think it would be helpful for the worship session.

TO SET THE SCENE

Brainstorm distinctives such as the gospel message of forgiveness, community not based on people's similarities and interests but on God's grace, hope for the future built on the certainty of God's word. Use this exercise to discuss how well the church presents this uniqueness or whether we have got used to downplaying what are actually our strengths.

1. The Israelites were impatient. Moses had been on Mount Sinai talking to God for forty days. They had quickly forgotten God rescuing them out of Egypt, they wanted instant answers and soon lost faith in Moses' leadership and Moses' God.

2. The Israelites were pleased with their god because they could see it, know where it was, and it helped them regain a sense of control. They did not need to wait on this god, he had no standards to adhere to, he was a tame god who did not punish their immorality.

4. If we edit God's holiness they we are editing the essence of his character. If he is not holy he is not 'other,' he is just like us. He would not be angry at sin, he would not be interested in purity, his love would have no power and merely be sentimental, he would be a man-made romantic notion of a manageable god.

5. Ideas could include preaching more about God's holiness, his hatred of sin and Jesus' death on the cross to pay the penalty for that sin; singing more hymns and songs about God's holiness; being more reverential in how we approach God in our prayers and worship times; including times of repentance and reflection so people can feel the weight of sin, its offence to a holy God, the cost of our forgiveness and our appropriate response of gratitude.

6. When we become Christians – trusting in Jesus' death for forgiveness of sins – we become holy in God's eyes. Jesus' once and for all sacrifice means that when God looks at us, he sees Christ's purity and not our sin. In a legal sense we are justified before God and we are set apart for his service.

7. Becoming holy in our actions, attitudes and behaviour is an ongoing process. Becoming more like Christ is a life-long pursuit. We grow in our holiness as we allow God's word to purify and transform us and as we deliberately refuse sin room in our lives.

8. Holiness is about loyalty and obedience to God (1 Kgs. 18:16–46). Holiness is not outward rituals or pretence of piety but about doing what it right, fighting for justice, looking after the weak and oppressed (Is. 1:10–17). Holiness is not a one-off task but an integrated life pursuing God's values and priorities (Is. 58). Holiness has an outward focus on moral and social ethics and an inward focus on pursuing a faithful relationship with God (Mich. 6:8).

9. The sacrificial system of the tabernacle and temple taught the Israelites about God's demand for holiness and the need for them to be pure when they approached him. Perhaps they learnt more about God's holiness by his reaction to their sin. For example, God demanded the stoning of Achan and his family for stealing from him (Josh. 7:1–26). Uzziah was covered in leprosy because of his pride (2 Chr. 26:16–20) and Uzzah was struck down for daring to touch the Ark of the Covenant (2 Sam. 6:6–7). In all God's dealings with the people, they learnt about his otherness, and his holiness showed up their sinfulness.

10. When we see God for who he is, we start to realise how sinful we are. We can't make ourselves holy: we need to ask God to change us, to make us holy, to give us a longing for holiness. Meditating on Scripture, prayer and church attendance don't make us holy in themselves but God can use these disciplines to purify us, to keep us on track in a spiritual sense, to give us strength to resist temptation and motivate us to do good, if our hearts are receptive to him. Difficulties in our lives can also be used by God to help us rely more on him and to develop our relationship with him.

SESSION 4

MATERIALS NEEDED

Flip chart, pens and paper

CDs or tapes and a music system if you think it would be helpful for the worship session.

TO SET THE SCENE

Use this exercise to reflect on how inclusive your church is, whether it is appealing to a certain sector, or even unintentionally excluding a certain group of people. Being realistic about the make-up of the church and our own networks will help us evaluate how well we are imitating Jesus and the particular ways we need to become more inclusive.

1. Jesus was speaking to a Samaritan, which Jews did not do, and also talking to a woman, which was taboo. And this particular woman had an immoral past and was living with a man who was not her husband. The fact that she was getting water in the heat of the day would suggest she had been shunned by the town.

3. Jesus saw sinners as sick people and himself as the doctor. He suggests in Mark 2:15–17 that table fellowship was part of the compassionate restorative process that was needed. In Luke 7:31–35 Jesus refused to be drawn into religious games or submit to what some saw as religious orthodoxy. He challenged his critics to be more mature. In Luke 15:1–7 Jesus explained that a repentant sinner was worth having a party for. In Luke 19:7–10 Jesus insisted that table fellowship was worth it because those excluded by religion, like Zacchaeus the Gentile tax collector, could be part of God's family. Faith in Jesus meant even Gentiles could become 'sons of Abraham.'

4. At different stages of life 'table fellowship' will look different. It is anything that builds relationships, invests in another person, and demonstrates acceptance.

5. Introduce issues such as the need to value individuals rather than see them as evangelistic targets; the need to balance your desire to win others for Christ and the need to build up your own faith; the fact that the Holy Spirit will open people's hearts to the gospel and not us; the reality that we may be misunderstood by others but it is God alone we are pleasing; the wisdom of having another Christian to pray through these types of dilemmas with.

7. Try and come up with practical suggestions you could implement in your church. For example, to show children with learning disabilities are welcome, you could start a Celebrations Group – a group dedicated to them and catering for their needs, running during the service. To show children are valued, you could have a monthly birthday slot in the service where those with birthdays are prayed for. Causeway Prospects are an organisation who can help with any work with those with learning disabilities: www.prospects.org.uk

8. Discuss with the group different ways of introducing the gospel to children, the types of props you have found helpful, and alternative ways to explain difficult concepts. Talk together about the need to speak the gospel plainly to children rather than sugar-coating it; the need to avoid manipulating them or seeing them as simply a means to reach their parents and the need to have rigorous discipleship in place.

9. Be specific about your particular church.

SESSION 5

MATERIALS NEEDED

Flip chart, pens and paper

CDs or tapes and a music system if you think it would be helpful for the worship session.

TO SET THE SCENE

Use this exercise to introduce the idea of kingdom to people. As you brainstorm values and defining features of the UK, there may be elements of our culture you would like to disassociate yourself from and people's feelings of allegiance may vary. To some extent, our dissatisfaction with our earthly kingdom points us to the kingdom of God which does not disappoint us and where we will never feel uncomfortable.

1. The kingdom of God is in essence the gospel message (Mt. 4:23). The kingdom was ushered into the world by Jesus' first coming (Mk. 1:14–15). The kingdom is also something that will come – we pray for God's rule to be more and more established on the earth. Jesus' second coming will fully establish his kingdom (Mt. 6:9–10). Jesus taught that his kingdom was so valuable that other things were insignificant in comparison. So we should give up everything that prevents us gaining the kingdom (Mt. 13:44–46). The kingdom is not physical or geographical as the Jews had anticipated, but spiritual, God's rule established in our lives (Lk. 17:20–21).

2. The prophet Zechariah had predicted that the Messiah would come riding on a donkey and that is how Jesus entered Jerusalem. He was declaring himself as king. The donkey was used by royalty and it symbolised that Jesus' kingdom was one of peace and humility.

3. Encourage people to convey the 'now but not yet' aspect of the kingdom, the joy and spiritual nature of the kingdom seen all places where God's values are lived out – the important point is to avoid religious jargon.

4. Peace rather than aggression, humility rather than boastfulness, self-sacrifice rather than self-aggrandisement, building others up rather than envy or jealousy, prayerful readiness rather than ignorance of Christ's return – the list is endless.

5. Explain that the kingdom does not just come in church or where Christians are involved. The kingdom breaks into our world when God's values and character are displayed.

6. Jesus said that love of money would affect our loyalty to God (Mt. 6:4). Encourage the group to discuss other issues such as busyness, pride, materialism and comfort.

9. Help people to see personal application here. Many Christians suffer much sadness in life, many sacrifice greatly so God's kingdom can be extended. Knowing that God's kingdom will be consummated one day, that God will rule, helps us see our pain is worth it.

SESSION 6

MATERIALS NEEDED
Flip chart, pens and paper

CDs or tapes and a music system if you think it would be helpful for the worship session.

Bread and wine/juice if you are going to celebrate communion together.

TO SET THE SCENE
Perhaps ask a few people in advance to share some of the highlights of their Christian experience so far. Use this exercise to remind people that we are on a journey, we should be making progress in godliness, we are far from perfect, but God still uses us in his plans.

1. God sent John the Baptist to prepare for Jesus' mission (Mk. 1:2–4). God sent Jesus to bring salvation to humanity (Jn. 3:16–17). Jesus sent the Holy Spirit as our Counsellor (Jn. 16:7). God sent apostles and prophets (Lk. 11:49). We are sent to tell people the gospel (Mt. 9:37–38).

2. Jesus has sent us out into the whole world. We are to make disciples not just converts, they are to be baptised and taught to obey everything in the Bible. This means evangelism is not just saying a prayer or raising a hand at a meeting. Our role is to make fully devoted followers of Christ, a life long pursuit.

3. The church has a responsibility to teach new converts, to ground them in truth, to explain the fundamentals of the faith. This may mean a curriculum is developed but in addition attention to the individual's spiritual growth is needed. Providing mentors is one way to do this. We need to develop a context of accountability, encourage the new Christian to find out their spiritual gifts and get involved in ministry. Discipleship will also happen informally as the young Christian models the faith of those they see in church.

4. Even the key disciple-makers in the early church continued to be disciples. They were flawed, made mistakes and were still growing in their faith. For example, in Acts 15, Paul wouldn't give Mark a second chance and allow him to join the mission team, After a blazing row, Paul split from his missionary partner, Barnabas. In Galatians 2:11–13, Peter had accepted the Gentiles as believers because of their faith in Christ, but when Jews from the circumcision party (those who believed you had to be circumcised to be saved) were around, he distanced himself from the Gentile believers.

5. Question 4 should have introduced the concept that all followers of Christ are flawed and still learning what it means to be a disciple. All of the biblical heroes had baggage – Abraham tried to pretend his wife was his sister, David had an illegitimate child and had Bathsheba's husband murdered. God knows we are broken but he still wants to use us. In fact, our weakness showcases God's strength (2 Cor. 4:7). On a practical note, it might be wise to pray with someone or have an older Christian as a mentor to provide support and feedback as you begin serving God and testing your gifts.

6. Communion takes us back to the Passover where the sacrifice of a lamb meant that the angel of death passed over the Israelites. For us, Christ's sacrifice as the spotless lamb of God means we don't need to fear death, we have eternal life. Just as the Israelites experienced freedom from Egypt, communion celebrates what Christ has done to make us free.

7. Baptism symbolises our identification with Christ when we become a Christian. It portrays Christ's death and resurrection. We join with him, dying to sin and our old life of disobedience, and rising to live for God. The act of baptism reminds us that our salvation cost Christ his life and also that we, through the power of the Holy Spirit, are committing to die to self and selfish desires. Our aim now is to live to please Christ in all we do, submitting to his will

8. The church is in an interim period. We have been saved but not yet taken to heaven, the kingdom has come but not yet in all its fullness. Both communion and baptism help us look back to the completed work of Christ, giving us hope and a certainty of the glory that will come. In the middle of busy lives, these sacraments remind us that we are sinners saved by grace, we have been cleansed and forgiven, set free for service and a radical new lifestyle. Together we rehearse what God has done and remember our part in the story of salvation.

Endnotes

1   Jeff Lucas, *One People, Spring Harvest Study Guide 2007* (www.springharvest.org)
2   Alan Stibbs, *God's church* (Leicester: IVP, 1959)
3   Liam Goligher, *The Fellowship of the King* (Milton Keynes: Authentic media, 2003)
4   Lucy Moore, *Messy church* (Oxford: Barnabas publishing, 2006)
5   Chris Wright, *Living as the people of God* (Leicester: IVP, 1983)
6   Donald McCullough, *The Trivialisation of God* (Navpress, 1995)
7   Loralee Hagan, quoted in *Searching for a God to love*, Chris Blake (Word Press, 1999)
8   Op cit
9   Op cit
10 Jeremy McQuoid, *How to set your heart on fire* (Milton Keynes: Authentic media, 2006)
11 Op cit
12 George Barna, *Transforming Children into Spiritual Champions* (Ventura CA: Regal Books, 2003)
13 Bill Hybels, *Just walk across the room: simple steps pointing people to faith* (Grand Rapids: Zondervan, 2006)
14 John Ortberg, *Everyone's normal until you get to know them* (Grand Rapids: Zondervan, 2003)
15 Roy McLoughry, *The eye of the needle* (Leicester: IVP, 1990)
16 Op cit
17 Vaughan Roberts, *God's big picture: tracing the story-line of the Bible* (Leicester: IVP, 2004)
18 Graeme Goldsworthy, *The Goldsworthy Trilogy* (Carlisle: Paternoster press, 2000)
19 Op cit
20 T M Moore, *Pastoral ministry and the place of the sacraments in Reforming pastoral ministry*, John H Armstrong, ed. (Wheaton: Crossways, 2001)
21 *The Apostolic Tradition* is an early manual of Christian church life and discipline which includes early forms of worship. It was formerly known as the 'Egyptian Church Order' but is now held to be the work of the third century Roman theologian Hippolytus (http://en.wikipedia.org/wiki/Apostolic_Tradition)
22 Robert Coleman *The masterplan of evangelism* (Revell. 1994)
23 Robert Coleman, *The masterplan of discipleship* (Revell, 1999)
24 John Ortberg, *The life you've always wanted* (Grand Rapids: Zondervan, 2004)